Eighteen Hummingbirds

Eighteen Hummingbirds

Quotes *and* Poetry | *A gift from the universe*

Trisha M. Holland

Copyright © 2018 by Trisha M. Holland /Holland Hummingbird Group
hollandhummingbirdgroup@gmail.com

Authored by: Trisha M. Holland
Editor/Friend: Maria Tucker
Advisor/Friend: Dale Smith Thomas
Cover and Interior Design: Bill Kersey, KerseyGraphics

Holland Hummingbird Group, LLC

ISBN: 978-0-692-03591-7

Dedication

Dedicated to the believers of the universe. You know who you are. To my family and to our loves that are now part of our universe's energy. Donna, Richard, Annie, Brandon, Holland, Joanna and our beautiful extended and bonus families.

To the communities of Summertown and Ethridge located in Lawrence County, Tennessee. My parents were so proud to be a part of your lives and have all of you be a part of ours.

To LaLa who saved my life.

To KTS and all my friends who loved their departed fur babies unconditionally as family. They forever live on.

To RMB #36 is with you always.

Thank you to the "bling team" for all the love.

There are too many best friends to mention that have encouraged me. They've had my back, wiped my tears, made a beauty queen out of me and made me laugh out loud. (way before LOL was a thing)

Author's Note

As my mother's time on this earth was coming to an end, I wondered how I would know that she was at peace.

My mother loved hummingbirds. The few that I had seen in my life were always in her presence. I wondered if I would be able to feel her sweet presence after she had gone. I knew her energy would be with the hummingbirds.

Around 3 am, she drew her last breath on a Monday in September.

My family and I left the hospital and I returned to my apartment an hour or so after sunrise. As I opened my door and walked onto my deck to feel the sun on my face, tears immediately filled my eyes. At least, eighteen hummingbirds swirled above my head and playfully darted among the trees.

Three old hummingbird feeders had been hung on a balcony directly above mine. Leaving the hospital every day after dark, I had not noticed a new neighbor had moved in and hung the feeders.

I ran into my neighbor in the parking lot. Tearfully, I told him the story about my mom. He confessed that the story didn't sound crazy to him at all as his father also loved hummingbirds.

As we talked, he explained that his father had passed away as well. Those three feeders on his deck had belonged to his father. They were always surrounded by a charm (or group) of hummingbirds. My neighbor had put these beautiful bright red feeders up in honor of his father and to watch one of nature's finest gifts.

That is how the universe works.

Standing on my deck, I could feel my mother's presence. I could feel her hugging me as the sweet hummingbirds floated on the breeze. And I knew, she was at peace.

The photograph for the Last Hummingbird was taken by my dear friend Vicky. My mother passed away on Vicky's birthday. Vicky said she was honored that mom picked a special day to join the hummingbirds. She gave me a print of this photo as a gift when mom died. I lost this amazing photographer and friend 2 years after I lost mom. Vicky was 57 years young. One of the last days I spent with her, she told me how beautiful she knew her next journey would be. The word journey is tossed around a lot, but I was comforted by her words. She is forever in my heart.

I have taken a nod from the universe. I'm sharing my quotes, poems and photographs.

Enjoy.

The Last Hummingbird

Sometimes I see one two three then four

I dread the cold when I see no more

The hum of the sweet song that you play

Comforts me as the dawn breaks

Spread your tiny wings

Float on the breeze

Surround yourself in warmth and ease

I will see you in spring

When you take flight

Surprise me

In a new season's sunlight

tmh

Sinking Ball of Fire

It's not just a sunset

Disappearing into the water

It's not just a sunset

Glistening like fire

It's the end of a day

That was given to you

You may have been smiling

Or singing the blues

It's the close of the hours that pass so fast

As the night falls

The day becomes the past

If a ray of the sun

Reveals itself tomorrow

Your heart has a chance to shed all its sorrow

Drink in the light

But prepare for rest

It's never just a sunset

tmh

Let go of what needs to sail in a different wind

tmh

A House

It was just a house

That held the chairs

Where we sat talked laughed and cried

It was just a house

Where she read her books

About mystery suspense and lies

It was just a house

Where we would visit

To give her flowers and peach pie

Now she's with the hummingbirds

Her home is the southern sky

tmh

Weightless

When we think we have life figured out
When we know there is little doubt
When the steadiness of the heart pounds
When there is little else to think about
The winds of change blow

When we're certain the days will pass the same
When we feel that we have won the game
When we need each hour to keep us sane
When we finally learn to embrace the rain
The winds of change blow

Wind becomes the breath of life
We breathe it in for only a while
The direction of the winds will shift
Let it lift us weightless
Accepting the change the wind brings us

toni

The Shallow End

For the people of Tortola, BVI

Some days overwhelm you

Others leave you wanting

In between are the hours

When the shadows seem haunting

In a dream you feel the water

Rising to your chin

You wake to realize

Your breath will start again

Some days you will see with a dry eye

Other days your eyes will weep

Today you stand in the shallow end

Tomorrow you will tread the deep

tmh

Ashes of A Soul

At the oceans edge

Sat down in the sand

Replayed every memory

I can still feel your hands

It hurts deep inside to know

That I'm letting go

Letting go of everything but your soul

I watched you float away

On the water and the wind

Your last breath took the pain away

Your spirit's home again

It hurts deep inside to know

That I'm letting go

Letting go of everything but your soul

On a rainy day when I'm alone

I can't even write a song

I'll hear your favorite melody

My heart will know for certain

Your soul didn't let go of me

tmh

The day we let go

*You may believe that angel wings belong
to the souls that moved on
I believe they should embrace the living
souls that feel alone*

tmh

The Leaf

On the trees outside my window

A few still hang

In hope and resilience

Through wind and rain

Some see an ending

I just see change

A chance to rebuild

New life forms again

Embrace the leaf

That floats to the earth

Becoming part of the soil

For growth and rebirth

tmh

Heart Beat

What does it mean when a heart skips a beat

Are you blue for a moment

Or just swept off your feet

It's a tiny interruption of your life line

While each breath you take is still on time

What does it mean when a heart skips a beat

Is it troublesome or a great relief

A sign of problems or true belief

Only the heart knows why it takes a pause

Then rushes life in again

No matter the cause

tmh

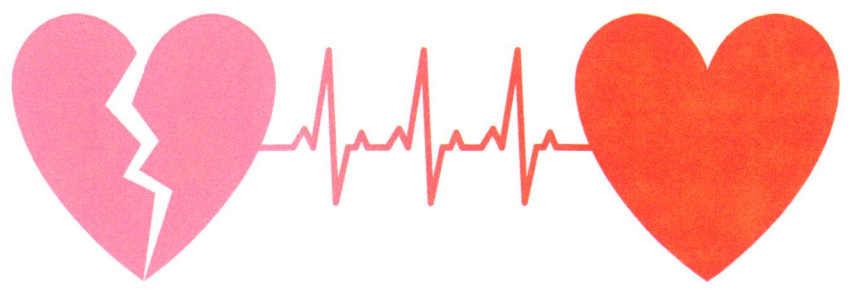

There is life on both sides of a sunset

tmh

Ask

Wait

Listen

Be Thankful

(for whatever the answer is...it is yours to trust)

tmh

Believe the universe when it shows you it's plan
The mystery will solve itself

tmh

The eighteenth is the day of the month my mother, sister and nephew were born. My sister married her love on the eighteenth. The eighteenth was the day of the month my daddy passed away. The date my mother died adds up to eighteen. 9-3-2013. The date my father died adds up to eighteen. 1-18-2015. The year my dad was born adds up to eighteen. 1935. Mother's cremation number adds up to eighteen. 1692. I could go on but, you get it. Sometimes, life just doesn't add up. Sometimes, it does.

It is never the end.

What was I thinking? Sometimes I write without thinking much about what will show up on the page. But this book is a compilation of quotes, poems and lyrics that I couldn't help but think about. They were swift to arrive in my head and had purpose. I believe the universe delivered them to me.

I do dread the cold when I might not be visited by hummingbirds. But I feel my mom around all the time now. The hummingbirds were just to help me on my way. I believe that letting go is a good thing. Keep what you need and shed things that don't have good energy. I wrote Ashes of a Soul while I was in my car. I was headed to Florida to spread Meemee's (mom's) ashes and sing those lyrics as we sent her out into the water.

If you have ever cleaned out a house of a parent that is no longer with you, then you know why I wrote A House. I couldn't bring myself to write about the house my dad lived in when he passed away. I grew up in that house. A lot of memories left to write about from that house.

Mom's house was just where we visited her. Her eyes told a different story of where her real home was.

I was on vacation when I took the photo of the sinking fishing boat. In front of me was a small abandoned sinking boat, and, in the distance, I could see very large expensive boats. One day those big boats could be in the shallow waters. I think we are all just trying to stay afloat.

Weightless was written for my friend Maggie. Her dad passed away. The changes that death brings are inevitable and I didn't want her to feel buried under the weight of them.

Sinking Ball of Fire came to me as I watched the sun's flames being snuffed out by the water. I thought, wow, another day gone and if I'm lucky I get to prepare for tomorrow. People often celebrate sunsets. It would be great if our sorrows disappeared with the sun each day. My sisters and I were sending a toast to our family members that had gone on to see the other side of the sunset when our friend Dawn took the photo.

Thank you, Donna and Annie for always supporting me and my words that spill out into the world.

Photograph Credits

Christy Long Photography: Cover photo - Murfreesboro, TN
Vicky Tubb Photography: The Last Hummingbird and
There is life on both sides of a sunset

Dawn Chapman Whitty Photography: Sinking Ball of Fire: "The Sistah Mermaids"
Donna Matthews and Annie Lockamy. Grayton Beach, Florida

Trisha M. Holland: The Shallow End - Tortola, BVI

Carmen Anne Tanner: Let go of what needs to sail in a different wind.
Michael Richardson: Graphic art design: Heart Beat

Annette McNamara Photography: Back cover/Socials page
Bill George: HHG logo design
Bethany K. Hullett: My rock star hair: Rock Your Locks
Donna Matthews: Zee Jewelry Designs: Jewels: Back cover/Socials page

Please join Trisha on her socials

trisha holland   hollandtrishal

www.ingramcontent.com/pod-product-compliance
Lightning Source LLC
Chambersburg PA
CBHW061822290426
44110CB00027B/2950